LILY DEVEZE

CARCASSONNE

BONECHI

* * *

© Copyright 1996 by Casa Editrice Bonechi, Via Cairoli 18/b, Florence - Italy - Telex 571323 CEB - Fax (55)5000766
All rights reserved. No part of this publication may be reproduced without the written permission of the Publisher.
The cover, layout and artwork by the Casa Editrice Bonechi graphic artists in this publication are protected by international copyright.
Printed in Italy by Centro Stampa Editoriale Bonechi.
Translated by Michel Campbell

Photographs from the Archives of Casa Editrice Bonechi taken by Luigi Di Giovine,
with the exception of photographs on pages:
9 below, 11, 19, 35, 41, 43, taken by Paolo Giambone.

ISBN 88-7009-974-1

A LITTLE HISTORY

Over a period of twenty centuries Nature, Art and History have combined to create an absolutely unique structure, the Citadel, not an isolated fortress but a fortified town standing on guard on the top of the cliff overlooking the river Aude. The river separates the Upper Town from the Lower Town. The latter, a modern town of about 46,000 inhabitants, nevertheless dates from the time of St. Louis. Romans, Visigoths, Saracens, Franks, feudal lords, seneschals and kings of France have all contributed their stone to the edifice to create this magnificent ensemble, the gateway to the Pyrenees and the sentinel of the historic corridor along which for centuries the flood of invasions has ebbed and flowed from the Mediterranean to Aquitaine and from Spain to the banks of the Loire. The Citadel is a book of stone in which to read the history of every period, and especially from which to learn about systems of military architecture from the Romans to the 14th century. The Romans settled here during the second century before the Christian era. Initially they set up an observation post and defense works, a castellum of average importance, on the site of an ancient celtic oppidum of the tribe of the Volces Tectosages. Later a colony of Roman veterans settled around the fort. This was the beginning of the town which over the centuries spread until it surrounded the fortifications from south-west to north-east. The records of Imperial Rome mention the existence of the «Colonia Julia Carcaso» in the year

20 B.C. Carcassonne enjoyed the benefits of the Pax Romana for the next four centuries. It was only when the barbarian hordes started to overrun the frontiers of the empire on the banks of the Rhine that the emperors ordered that the cities of the interior should repair their fortifications or, if they did not already have any, that they should construct some. After the fall of Rome, Carcassonne fell to the Visigoths. They used the city as a base for their operations, an enormous headquarters which they occupied for nearly 300 years from about 440 A.D. until 725 A.D. During this period they restored the ramparts. However in 725 A.D. came the sudden violent invasion by the Saracens. These Moslems from Spain have left memories and legends rather than buildings. Not even the Pinte Tower can claim to be of this period. With Charles Martel the Christian cause triumphed again and the Carolingian Franks became all powerful. Charlemagne's Empire having shifted its southern frontier into Catalonia, the Citadel lost something of its military importance and there does not appear to have been any important event concerning it during this period.

It was only after the death of the Emperor Charlemagne and following the rapid disintegration of his Empire that the local representatives of the central government became gradually independent. This marked the beginning of the feudal period during which the counts and viscounts of Carcassonne

General view of the Citadel from the north-west

Panorama of the Citadel, south-east side

ruled without interruption for three centuries. The counts, in particular Roger le Vieux and the dynasty of the Trencavels, lived in the Citadel itself. The major achievement of the Trencavels was the construction of the castle and of the Romanesque nave of the Basilica of St. Nazaire. Contrary to what is often said there was a considerable amount of travel in the Middle Ages and commerce flourished in the region thanks to commercial exchanges with the Middle East. It was these very exchanges which led to the introduction in the 11th century of the doctrine known as Catharism or Albigensianism. This doctrine is based on an oriental dualism which has as its principal characteristics, on the one hand, the God of Good, creator of everything concerned with the spirit, and on the other, the principal of Evil, creator of the visible world, and thus of man, and also of matter and of everything which has a terrestrial existence. This doctrine was very severe. So austere indeed was it that only the initiates who had received the «consolamentum», the only sacrament of this doctrine, could practice it. This elite constituted by the initiates, called the Pure or Perfects, from the Greek noun «catharos» (pure), formed the major part of the clergy of the sect. In contrast the sympathisers and believers could live as they thought fit but, when they were thought to be in danger of dying, they received, the sacrament of consolamentum.

When the Crusaders from the North of France poured over the South with the intention of exterminating the Cathars or Albigensians, the Citadel of Carcassonne held out against the assault and Raymond-Roger Trencavel resisted all alone the attack of the northern barons. Only lack of water and treachery delivered him into the hands of Simon de Montfort on the 15th August 1209. In 1229 St. Louis took up the Crusade. In 1240 the feudal Citadel was once again subjected to a terrible seige when the son of Trencavel came to attack the conquerors from beyond the Loire (the Northerners). He failed, but after the seige St. Louis realized that the Citadel needed more solid defenses. He undertook to strengthen considerably this spot so close to the southern frontier of his kingdom. His builders started by constructing the outer wall around the inner wall. The walls were furnished at the points of access to the city with demilune outworks known as «barbicans», flanked by numerous towers which for the most part commanded little or no view on the curtains in order not to hinder the fire from the inner wall. The construction of the outer defences more than doubled the protection of the defence works which they surrounded since any enemy was obliged to surmount two obstacles in place of one. However it was Philip the Bold, son of St. Louis, who from 1270 to 1285 gave the Citadel its full development and its royal defence works. Military art

4

had evolved and had reached its pinnacle in defensive fortifications. Between the two lines of defences the sloping terrain was levelled in order to create the Lists. During these excavations it was necessary to use the Roman and feudal foundations of the inner defences as underpinning for the new building which explains why the towers are built on top of some 13th century royal architecture.

The Basilica of St. Nazaire and St. Celse is a miraculous blending of two styles of architecture, feudal and royal, as is shown by the remarkable harmony between the Romanesque nave and the Gothic transept and choir. Under the royal government the Citadel had become impregnable. The defence works of the fortress are so formidable that when the Black Prince, son of Edward III of England, swept through the south during the Hundred Years War, he burnt down the Lower Town built by St. Louis but left the Citadel alone. However the Pyrenean Treaty in the 17th century destroyed Carcassonne's strategic importance by moving the frontier between France and Spain right up to the Pyrenees. The inevitable decline of Carcassonne followed. In 1791 the Citadel was reduced to the rank of a third class fortified town and in 1806 it was removed completely from the list of fortified towns. In 1836 Jean-Pierre Cros-Mayrevieille of Carcassonne, who had an intense love for his native town, and the man who really saved the Citadel,

drew the attention of the French government to the state of the monuments in the Citadel. He continued to clamour for their restoration over a period of many years. Repair work on the Basilica of St. Nazaire was started in 1840. However in 1850 for financial reasons the Prince-President, the future Napoleon III, struck the Citadel off the list of historical monuments. Cros-Mayrevieille with the support of the Société des Arts et Sciences and of the Municipal Council succeeded in having the decree rescinded, and the Citadel was returned to the control of the Ministry of National Defence and classified once again as a fortified town. Prosper Mérimée, when he became Inspector General of Historical Monuments, undertook a tour of inspection in the south during which he visited Carcassonne. He immediately sent an urgent appeal to Paris, as a result of which Viollet-le-Duc, who had been alone in supervising the work on the church since 1844, was finally given the responsibility in 1853 of carrying out 'restoration work and consolidation on the towers and ramparts of the Citadel under the direction of the Committee for Historical Monuments of the Ministry of the Interior'. The restoration of the Citadel by Viollet-le-Duc gave rise to considerable discussion. Nevertheless it is in fact one of the least contestable restorations carried out by this great architect. Thanks to his great enthousiasm a unique monument has been preserved.

Aerial view of the Citadel taken from the north.

West side of the Citadel illuminated and panorama of the Citadel and the Pont Vieux seen from the Pont Neuf.

The two Narbonne Towers which flank the principal gateway to the east. On the right is the Tresau Tower while in the foreground are the draw-bridge and the moat.

THE PONT VIEUX

The old bridge dates more or less from the period during which the Lower Town was built by St. Louis, i.e. from the period 1247-1260. Its appearance is very similar to that of the Pont Saint-Esprit on the Rhone. It is 210 metres long and has a average width of 5 metres. However in the special wide points known as «becs» or beaks which constitute a kind of refuge for pedestrians it has a width of 9 metres. Its 12 round arches are of unequal width, the largest being 14 metres wide, the narrowest only 10 metres. A cross placed in the third of these pedestrian refuges is a reminder of the arch which formally marked the boundary between the two communities, that of the Upper Town and that of the Lower Town.

THE NARBONNE GATE

The Narbonne Gate is the principal point of entry to the Citadel and is so called because it faces east towards the town of Narbonne. It consists of twin towers flanking the gateway and joined by a building constructed above the latter. The gates having been the most vulnerable points of fortified medieval towns it is no surprise to find that even by the standards of the time this one is exceptionally strong.

Various structures preceded the Narbonne Gate but the one which we now have before our eyes is undoubtedly one of the most beautiful which still survive from the Middle Ages. The towers are about 25 metres high and the thickness tapers from about 4 metres at the base to about 2.80 metres higher up.

THE EXTERIOR OF THE NARBONNE TOWERS

The Narbonne towers, which defend the only carriageable gateway to the Citadel were constructed in about 1280, during the reign of Philip the Bold, and are built of those beautiful rough-hewn blocks of sandstone which were used in this period. These rough blocks of stone were less vulnerable than the others inasmuch as projectiles tended to bounce off them. The defences of the towers included on the outside a spur something like the prow of a ship. At the base this spur increases the resistance at the precise point which is most exposed to mining operations while higher up it improves the line of fire from the 'hoardings'. Furthermore it gave to the defenders posted on the curtains a better angle of vision from which to discover any pioneers in the process of attacking the base of the towers. As far as the gate itself was concerned its defence was assured by a plethora of precautions. Firstly a chain was strung across the gateway to break the impetus of the cavalry. Then there was a machicoulis, a kind of opening in the vaulting of the gateway for dropping stones and other projectiles, and immediately after there was a portcullis. One can still see the grooves in which the portcullis slid up and down. Behind this portcullis there was an iron-shod door, then a central machicoulis, a kind of trap known as the 'assomoir' (bludgeon). There follow a third machicoulis, a second door and a second portcullis. The defences outside the gate are the moat, the draw-bridge and the barbican, whose entrance is cut on the bias thus forcing the assaillants to present their flank to the defenders.

THE LEGEND OF LADY CARCAS

The statue of this legendary heroine stands in front of the drawbridge. Lady Carcas was the wife of the Saracen king Balaack. Charlemagne having laid siege to Carcassonne was determined to reduce the town by famine. The siege lasted five years, by the end of which the entire garrison had died of hunger. Lady Carcas then made some dummies which she arranged all along the ramparts and spent her days shooting arrows at the enemy camp. She let the only

The Narbonne outer gate, the draw-bridge and the two Narbonne towers.

Top: Bust of Lady Carcas with the inscription «SUM CARCAS».
Bottom: View down onto the draw-bridge.

pig she had left eat all her remaining grain and when it was thoroughly stuffed she threw the animal down from the top of a tower. Its belly was ripped open by the fall and spilt out a large quantity of ill-digested wheat grain, with the result that Charlemagne, discouraged, decided to lift the seige. However Lady Carcas was satisfied with the glory of having defeated the great Charlemagne by a ruse and sounded the trumpets to call him back. He did not hear the sound of the trumpets but his esquire said to him «Sire, Carcas te sonne» ('Sire, Carcas is calling you'). From this, it is claimed, comes the name of the town.

THE INTERIOR OF THE NARBONNE TOWERS

After our brief survey of the outside of these imposing towers we shall now examine their interior defences. It should be stressed that in the 13th century the towers were completely self-contained. On the inside, the town side, the towers are flat and are linked by a massive wall, so as to appear as a single piece of masonry. The tower on the same side as the 'Tresau' or Treasure tower, the left, is called the North tower and the other is called the South tower. The room on the ground floor might be called the «Slaughter house» since the garrison kept their meat and provisions there, in a vast cellar whose square entrance may still be seen. There they would have salted pork and beef, grain, beans, oil, a vast quantity of salt and, of course, wine. There are four loop-holes or arrow-slits in the wall which looks out onto the Lists and two others which give onto the vaulted passageway. On the left a stair leads up to the first floor.

The ground floor room in the North tower might be called the «cistern room» since it contained a cistern having a capacity of about a hundred cubic metres, which would have been kept filled with rain water brought in by lead or terracotta pipes. There was also a system for emptying the tank to permit it to be cleaned. This involved emptying the water into the moat.

This room also has six arrow slits, of which one lies along the edge of the projecting spur. The hooks above the arrow slits may have been used by the soldiers for hanging up their cross-bows or possibly, according to a more recent theory, for hanging the shutters to close the slits. On the first floor each tower has a door giving onto the way patrolled by the sentries. The first floor rooms are very much alike. They are vast and handsome and each has a fire-place and an oven. The arches of the vaults are supported by interesting and varied corbels. Between these two rooms there is a small room whose only function is to defend the gateway. The second floor is not internally divided and forms one vast hall lighted by five Gothic windows giving onto the town. It is known as the «Knights' Hall». There is a third floor under the eaves. To sum up, each of the Narbonne towers is organised so that it can withstand a long siege on its own.

The passage between the Narbonne towers
The statue of the Virgin (late 13th century) above the Narbonne Gate.

Several views of the towers of Narbonne.

View of the east side of the castle seen from inside the Citadel.　　　　View of the entrance to the castle flanked by two towers. ▶

THE CASTLE

Viollet-le-Duc thought that it was constructed about 1130. In that case the castle would have been built by Bernard Aton Trencavel, the founder of the dynasty, or by his son Roger III. It was here that the Viscounts Trencavel lived and it was here that Raymond-Roger Trencavel died as a prisoner in 1209. Afterwards Simon de Montfort established his headquarters in the castle. Under the monarchy it was the residence of the seneschals. They were charged with the administration of the royal domain under the authority of a governor who was the direct representative of the king. During the Ancien Régime the castle was also used for the detention of young men whose bad conduct their parents wanted to punish. In the 19th century the castle became a barracks and during the First World War about 300 German officers were imprisoned there. In March 1944 the Germans took over the Citadel in order to use it as their headquarters and the inhabitants were obliged to leave their homes, to which they returned again on 20th August 1944 after the Liberation.

During the Middle Ages the castle was the ultimate refuge, a fortress within a fortress. The three facades, to the east, to the north and to the south, relied for their protection on the science of the builder. On these three sides its walls defined a perfect rectangle. The stout walls are furnished with battlements in which alternate embrasures are pierced with a long narrow arrow-slit through which one can shoot with a bow. On the east side there are 5 towers, cylindrical on the outside and flat on the inside. They are each divided into four floors and the circular rooms of the ground floor and the first floor have vaulted ceilings in the shape of a cupola or hemispherical cap. There are two rows of arrow-slits in the curtains and the towers have arrow-slits on every floor. These arrow-slits are cut on the bias in order not to weaken the masonry. According to Raymond Ritter, in this castle at Carcassonne, where the great feudal military architecture had its origins, one finds all the principal defensive measures which continued to constitute up until the 16th century, with a greater or lesser degree of adaptation or improvement, the basic ABC of the military builder.

View of the east side of the castle. On the right one can see the hoardings at the top of the ramparts and of the tower.

EAST SIDE OF THE CASTLE AND ITS DEFENCES

Approaching the castle from the east the first thing one sees is the gateway of a semicircular barbican which used to stand in front of the moat. This gate still has its defences. First of all the enormous hinges which used to support a two-leaf wooden door and then arrow-slits and battlements furnished with shutters. The upper part of the barbican was open on the castle side in order to prevent the assaillants using it against the castle if it fell into their hands. This barbican within the town was built during the reign of St. Louis to protect the approaches to the castle against either an eventual uprising by the inhabitants of the town or against an enemy who had managed to gain a footing within the Citadel. The moat was in the past much deeper but did not contain water. It simply served to prevent the approach of engines of war. Originally the stone bridge finished about two metres before the gate at the entrance to the castle and the two were joined by means of a movable wooden bridge. The use of a drawbridge did not become generalised until the 14th century. All along the east side of the castle we can still see two rows of square holes, called putlog holes, for the installation of a sort of wooden gallery. When one notes how extremely narrow the sentry-ways are and the impossibility for the men at arms to defend the foot of the ramparts without sticking their bodies half out, one readily appreciates the need to do something about it. Therefore stout beams were placed in the square holes at the level of the sentry-way. At the end of the beams on the outer side were fitted sloping beams connected together with planks. Flooring was laid on top of the main beams, with a gap left in the planking, so as to make it into a sort of machicoulis. There was a roof above the whole thing. These galleries or 'hoardings' which you can see in the pictures on pages 14 and 15, have been reconstructed from the drawings of Viollet-le-Duc. The advantage of the hoardings was that they enabled the defenders to stand outside the battlements with a commanding view of the base of the battlements and yet be completely sheltered. Supplies were built up on the sentry-ways, from where they were passed to the outside through the embrasures which served as doors. The round arch between the two towers which flank the entry gate hides a machicoulis behind which there stands a first portcullis and wooden doors. As a further precautionary measure there was again a second portcullis backed by another machicoulis and a second door.

Top: The castle barbican within the town.

Bottom: The west side of the castle seen from the great courtyard. The Archeological Museum is on the first floor.

The west side of the castle with in the foreground «la Grande Caponniere» (a caponier is a covered passage across a dry moat).

THE TOWERS ON THE WEST SIDE AND THE DEFENCES ON THE RIVERSIDE OF THE AUDE

The «Grande Caponnière» or covered passage was a battlemented stairway of which a part still survives. This fortified passage went as far as the great tower of the Barbican built by St. Louis on the site of an even older fortification. The Barbican was demolished in 1816 and Viollet-le-Duc built St. Gimer there on part of the site in about 1850. The caponier connected the Citadel with the Barbican, whose function it was to protect the approach to the Citadel on the side towards the river. We know that the river used to flow much closer to the Citadel than it does today. After the foundation of the township or lower town St. Louis altered the course of the river and drained the marshes. Today the Aude flows about half-way between the lower town and the Citadel.

In the photo above you can see the west side of the castle which is built on top of the Gallo-Roman ramparts. From left to right: the Powder Tower, which dates from the 13th century, the bartizan or watch-tower, the pseudo-donjons, the Pinte Tower and on the extreme right-hand side the Justice To-

wer. It is indeed rather remarkable that the castle does not have a true keep or donjon given that at the time of its construction keeps had become common-place to the north of the Loire. The builders contented themselves with constructing on top of the Gallo-Roman foundations a rectangular tower with the longer face outwards, the Pinte or 'Pinto' Tower. This tower, which is 28 metres high, was a watch-tower one of whose functions was the transmission of signals. Viollet-le-Duc found that it had all the characteristics of the Romanesque period, so that the possibility that it dates from the Saracens can be ruled out. It doubtless belongs to the first phase in the construction of the castle (1130) and is not vaulted. It was originally divided into ten levels by wooden floors, which have all disappeared so that it is now impossible to reach the top of the tower. The floors were no doubt connected by wooden stairways or ladders. An old story recounts that the Pinte Tower 'doffed its hat' before the Emperor. This legend is mentioned in the «Chronicle of Charlemagne» which is attributed to Turpin. Between the Powder Tower and the castle watch-tower there is an archway, beneath which is the West Gate of the castle. Access to the castle was limited by the outer walls and the only two gates were the West Gate and another on the east side which is actually inside the town.

17

The twin towers at the entrance gate.
The castle sentry-way sheltered by the roof of the 'hoardings'.

THE CASTLE EAST GATE TOWERS AND THE TRENCAVEL PRIVATE APARTMENTS

The inside of the gate towers forms a homogeneous whole similar to that of the Narbonne Towers. However communication between the upper and lower floors was only possible by means of wooden ladders on the inside of the flat wall facing onto the courtyard. Passage from the second floor to the first floor was through a trap-door in the vaulting. In this part of the defence works, as in all the towers and gates in the outer walls and inside the castle, everything has been arranged so that the officers in charge of military operations can reach the points at which the means of defence are deployed from above. It therefore comes as something of a surprise to see on the second floor of such an austere building a beautiful double window in the Romanesque style.

The south side of the courtyard is occupied by a building which separates the great courtyard from the small inner courtyard. This building includes the great hall, the lord's apartments, and the kitchens, which are in the basement.

In the centre of the great courtyard must once have stood the feudal elm, a symbolic tree which is often mentioned in the writings of the period. It was here in all probability that were held the assemblies of the Court of Love presided over by Adelaide de Burlats, daughter of the Count of Toulouse, wife of Roger Trencavel and mother of the unfortunate Raymond-Roger Trencavel, victim of the Albigensian Crusade.

The Pinte Tower seen from the small inner courtyard of the castle.

Archeological Museum, first room: the Roman finds.

Funerary head, marble,
Gallo-Roman period.

Funerary terracotta,
Gallo-Roman period.

ARCHEOLOGICAL MUSEUM – GALLO-ROMAN ROOM

This museum, which is inside the castle, and of whose holdings we shall only mention a few items, is made up in large part of two collections. Firstly there is the Viollet-le-Duc Collection, consisting of a series of original sculptures from the Basilica of St. Nazaire and dating from the 12th to the 14th centuries, together with casts taken from the originals and models made under the direction of Viollet-le-Duc for the restoration of the internal and external sculptures of this church. The other major collection consists of a number of objects of great interest, all of local origin, purchased by the Société des Arts et des Sciences de Carcassonne.

The most beautiful item in the so-called Roman Room is the 4th century sarcophagus of Tournissan. Behind it can be seen the mile-stone of Numerian, 'prince of youth'. At the back one can see some amphorae and the stones from some oil presses. On the right in the foreground there is a sarcophagus, from the Visigothic period to judge by its lid which is roof shaped.

Top: The Roman Room in the Archeological Museum.

Bottom: Tombstones (crosses).

THE ROMANESQUE ROOM OF THE ARCHEOLOGICAL MUSEUM

In the centre of the room can be seen one of its most beautiful items; a marble ablutionary basin from the 12th century. On the right against the wall is a paleo-christian sarcophagus on which are depicted a vine leaf and an ear of corn, symbols having great significance to early Christians. Behind the sarcophagus there is an antependium (veil for the front of the altar) which is elaborately decorated with interlaces and which comes from the Basilica of St. Nazaire. You will also notice some capitals from the North Door of St. Nazaire, and in the middle at the back the columns and capitals from the covered gallery in St. Nazaire known as the 'Inquisitors' Gallery'.

The tomb-stones or disc-shaped stele from the old cemeteries of the churches of St. Michel de Carcassonne and of the Lauragais (13th-14th centuries) have been the subject of much discussion. Some scholars have maintained that they are Cathar stele. According to the eminent specialist on the subject, professor René Nelli, only stele on which is depicted

The Villànière Calvary, front: Ecce Homo.
Back: The Annunciation.

the Greek Cross can be of Cathar origin since the Cathars adopted the Greek Cross in opposition to the Latin Cross in which they saw the instrument of torture of Christ. It is possible to find innumerable variations of these disc-shaped crosses in the Pyrenean region.

THE DONJON ROOM

The third room in the museum is the 'camera rotunda' or round room which is part of the big false keep. The archives frequently refer to this 'round room' even though it is in fact rectangular. It probably owes its name to its barrel vault. It was here that important documents were signed and it was here that the lord's court sat on important occasions. It is now a part of the museum and contains the Villanière Calvary, Villanière being a small hamlet near Carcassonne. It depicts the *Ecce Homo* on one side and the *Annunciation* on the other. It dates from the 16th century, prior to which the suffering Christ such as one sees here was not depicted in religious works. He was either represented in triumph or teaching as in the South Rose of the Basilica of St. Nazaire. On the back of the Calvary we find the Annunciation. At the top of the upright there are eight apostles. On the back of the cross are depicted the Virgin and Child between two saints. This ceremonial hall was formerly decorated with 12th century murals which were found and uncovered in 1926.

At this point it is impossible not to evoke that most engaging personality, Raymond-Roger Trencavel, Viscount of Carcassonne and Beziers, the great hero of Occitan Independence, who alone stood up to the onslaught of the northern knights in 1209 at the time of the Crusade against the Cathars or Albigensians. When he appeared at Montpellier before the Assembly of the Crusaders presided over by the Papal Legate, where he was invited to hunt down and then hand over the heretics in his towns, Raymond-Roger declared: 'I offer a town, a roof, a shelter, bread and my sword to all the outlaws who will soon be wandering about Provence with neither town, roof, shelter nor bread'. Alas, after the sack of Beziers and the massacre of the population, the Crusaders laid siege to Carcassonne on the 1st August 1209. The siege only lasted fifteen days, after which lack of water forced Raymond-Roger to leave the town and go the Crusaders' camp. We are led to the conclusion from reading the «Chanson de la Croisade Albigeoise» ('Song of the Albigensian Crusade') that Raymond-Roger went to parley not to surrender. Nevertheless the Crusaders made him prisoner and he died, still a prisoner, in one of his own towers in November 1209. He was not yet 25 years old.

Top: 12th century mural.

Bottom: Detail from the Villanière Calvary.

THE MURAL

This painting represents a French knight, the white rider, in combat with a Saracen knight carrying a round shield. It must be either a scene from «The Song of Roland», which was very much in vogue at this period even in the South of France, or an episode from the Spanish Crusade of Bernard Aton, founder of the Trencavel dynasty, who went to fight the Saracens. The episode must date from before 1170, since from this period on conical helmets such as that of the French knight were no longer worn. One is struck by the distinction of the horses and by the masterly way in which the clash of the two horsemen is drawn. Murals of the Romanesque period are very rare in Languedoc. Because of their great fragility paintings have always been very prone to destruction, and never has this been truer than for Languedoc in the Middle Ages.

Recumbent figure of a Knight on his tomb.

ROOM OF THE RECUMBENT KNIGHT

The fourth room which is devoted to the Gothic period contains this large 14th century effigy which comes from the Abbey at Lagrasse which was founded by Charlemagne. It also contains various key-stones including one with the effigy of St. Louis. There are also five raised tombs which come from the convents of the Cordeliers and of the Augustines in Carcassonne, as well as the basin of a fountain decorated with figures and little arches. Against the wall separating the two rooms there is a 14th century «smiling angel» with a vague resemblance to the «Smiling Angel» at Rheims Cathedral, although this one has been sculpted with less finesse and furthermore is mutilated. It was found in the Citadel during the work on the theatre.

Stone bas-relief showing six figures each framed in an arch, from the Basilica of St. Nazaire.

Arcade formed by three 14th century windows from the Maison Grassalio in the Lower Town.

THE ARCADE ROOM

The three Gothic windows above are quite remarkable. They can be dated by the coiffures of the figures in the arches. The Maison Grassalio used to stand on the spot where the Hotel des Postes now stands. The fourth window is still in the Lower Town opposite the main doorway to the present Cathedral of St. Michael. The smiling Virgin otherwise known as the Virgin with the bird is a very interesting 14th century statue which was purchased by the State with the help of the 'Amis de la Ville et de la Cité de Carcassonne'. Like all Gothic Virgins it lacks the rigidity of the Romanesque Virgins. The Virgin is here depicted as Wife and Mother rather than Queen. As she looks at her child her smiling face is full of love. The only thing to be regretted is that the Infant Jesus was decapitated during the French Revolution and his head has been replaced by another very different one.

Left: Statue of St. Basilice, stone, 14th century. *Right*: «The smiling Virgin» also known as «The Virgin with the bird».

Above: Case with English alabaster pieces dating from the 14th century: «The Flagellation», «Christ in Limbo», «Christ on the Cross» and «The Resurrection» all originating from the church of St. Sernin in the Citadel.

Below left: «The Flagellation».

Below right: «Christ on the Cross».

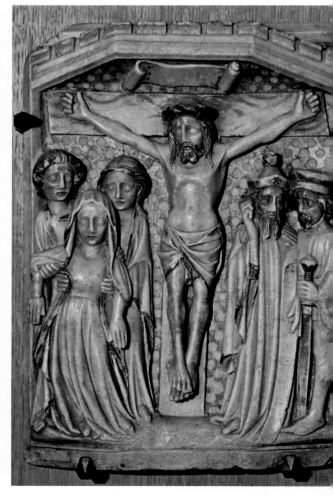

ST. SERNIN AND EARLY CHRISTIANITY

Christianity was practised in the province early on and St. Sernin or Saturnin, first Bishop of Toulouse, was martyred there round about the year 250. He was dragged through the town by a maddened bull and according to tradition the Eglise du Taur at Toulouse marks the spot where the bull finally came to a halt. The Basilica of St. Sernin in Toulouse was constructed over the saint's tomb.

There is also a church of St. Sernin in the Citadel and the oldest document in which it is mentioned is one from 1308 in which the Bishop of Rodier instituted the Brotherhood of St. Louis (la Confrérie de Saint-Louis) for the use of the Mortes-Payes. The church was demolished in 1793 by order of the administration. The church of St. Sernin formerly stood where the calvary which can be seen from the Place Marcou and which still bears its name now stands. A beautiful Gothic window in the Tower of St. Sernin's Sacraire, which stands beside the North Narbonne Tower, allowed light to fall on the apse of the church. In 1441 Charles VIII permitted this window to be enlarged. According to a long standing tradition St. Sernin was supposed to have been imprisoned in this tower.

«The Resurrection» also from the church of St. Sernin.

1 2

3 4

1) ST. PAUL'S TOWER

This tower stands at the south east corner of the castle. It can be reached from the small inner courtyard by means of a modern wooden staircase which has replaced the original stone spiral staircase. Inside the tower the rooms have admirable hemispherical or cupola vaulted ceilings typical of the 12th century.

2) THE GRAND BURLAS TOWER AND THE OUTER WALL

This tower stands at the south west extremity of the outer wall. Before the outer wall was constructed by St. Louis, it constituted the weakest point in the defences of the Citadel being ill-defended by nature.

3) ROMANESQUE CAPITAL

In the covered gallery known as «The Inquisitors' Gallery», which presumably linked the Justice Tower to the hall where the Inquisitors held session, there are three linked Romanesque windows. The capitals in the first and third windows have acanthus leaves round them. On that shown in the photograph there is a crouching man clutching to his breast with his right hand a somewhat ill-defined object in the shape of a crossed O.

5

6

4) THE ST. NAZAIRE TOWER

This tower has been extensively reconstructed. The older part includes the lower two floors specifically intended for the defence of the south postern and giving access to the Lists.

5) THE STEP TOWER

This tower interrupts the castle sentry-way on the north side. As in the towers at the main entrance the different floors were formerly connected by a wooden stairway on the outside. It provides an excellent view of the Lower Town.

6) THE INSIDE WALL, THE COVERED GALLERY, THE JUSTICE TOWER AND THE PINTE TOWER

Leaving the Justice Tower one passes through the «Inquisitors' Gallery» at the end of which there is a machicoulis situated just above the Aude Gate. At the bottom of the steps on the right there is the opening of a second machicoulis and then of a third.

SLOPE UP TO THE AUDE GATE

The way up to the Aude Gate starts near the modern church of St. Gimer. The path first climbs up the west escarpment of the Citadel and then right under the Petit Canissou Tower it makes a right-angle bend and turns north. At this point it becomes a fortified corridor with the Outer Wall on the right and a battlemented wall on the left. A depressed gate, followed by another dating from the 13th century, in tierce-point, constitute the Aude outer gate. Against the Inner Wall, which is on the right, there are some buttresses supporting the machicoulis defending the approach. The space where one now finds oneself, completely surrounded by battlements, would have been a death-trap to any attackers that got that far. There is a door at the foot of the Justice Tower, beyond which a stair leads in to the Aude Gate proper, this gate being overlooked by a machicoulis on consoles (a kind of masonry bracket).

Top: The way up to the Aude Gate with the Justice Tower and the castle in the background.

Below: South side of the castle.

THE SOUTH SIDE OF THE CASTLE

The St. Paul Tower is the only corner tower on the south side of the castle. The Pinte Tower, which can be seen on the left, is in the middle of the west curtain which runs along the small internal courtyard of the castle. In the Viscounts' time the latter had a broad portico on which St. Louis constructed a vast hall supported by a floor whose corbels can still be seen from inside the courtyard. This hall must have been either the fencing hall or the ceremonial hall. It would have been at this period that the beautiful Gothic window which can be seen in the photograph was let in to the south curtain. When the Festival of the Citadel is held, the small courtyard is used for theatre performances, concerts and ballet.

The outer defences of the castle known as "le grand Châtelet".

The impressive mass of the castle illuminated.

THE CITADEL PAST AND PRESENT

The first-time visitor to the Citadel is often surprised to discover that, inside, it is a living town. One comes expecting to find a castle and fortifications, and in this one is not disappointed. However having passed the Narbonne Gate one finds oneself in an intricate network of streets full of souvenir shops, antique dealers, bakeries, pastry shops, food shops, restaurants and hotels. In the summer these little streets with their tiny squares shaded by plane trees are the scene of intense activity. When night falls these apparently dead stones come to life and stimulate our imagination. What was the life of the inhabitants like under the Viscounts or under the Kings? Life must have been very active with the various artisans going about their business: some weaving the wool which their wives had spun on a distaff, the blacksmiths beating iron for the war horses, carpenters shaping beams of wood, the guilds of master-masons in their workshops. Agricultural life went on around the fortress and under its protection. The time of the Trencavels was the most brilliant period in the life of the Citadel, and the period which was distinguished by the lyric poetry of the Troubadors, but looking at it more closely one is surprised to find that it was also a period of civic independence and respect for the rights of the people which has no analogue before modern times. The Troubadors were received, lodged and fêted at the castle at any time of the year.

However by the 13th century the Citadel had become a Royal town and a frontier town and had assumed an almost exclusively military air. According to Viollet-le-Duc's calculations it would have required 1,323 men to defend the 48 towers and 4 barbicans. This takes account only of the fighting men and it is necessary to add to this the crews of the war machines and the workers, the number of whom must have been at least twice that of the combatants. Considering the length of perimeter of the Inner and Outer Walls, respectively 1100 and 1500 metres, we are drawn to the conclusion that there was one man per metre and that each tower or barbican was guarded by about twenty men while the castle itself would have had a garrison of 200 men and the Narbonne Gate would have been defended by about 50 men. At this period, then the Citadel was a garrison town with a population of about 4000. It is likely that the Lists or the space between the Inner and Outer Walls would have served for stocking materials, arms and timber. There must have been a tremendous amount of activity going on at any one time, when one thinks of the enormous amount of building work undertaken by the Kings of France and in particular of their efforts to make the Citadel impregnable.

The Way up to the Aude Gate with the Petit Canissou Tower dominated by the Justice Tower. On the right the Bishop's Square Tower.

The Aude Gate with the Machicoulis directly above.

THE JUSTICE TOWER

It was built in the 13th century to replace a Gallo-Roman tower and doubtless served as the Office of the Clerk to the Court of the Inquisition. It has no holes for the beams supporting a covered hoarding. In this way the risk of fire constituted by a wooden gallery under the eaves was avoided, and this was important since it was desired at all costs to protect the documents relating to cases against heretics. The room on the first floor shows no signs of any military apparatus. In the Six-ribbed Gothic Archway there are twelve hooks placed in pairs which probably served for hanging the leather bags in which the archives of the Inquisition were kept. The hall known as «the hall of the Inquisition», which still exists, was an annex to the tower.

Room on the second floor of the Tower of the Inquisition seen from the floor above.

THE TOWER OF THE INQUISITION

This circular room is lighted by two large windows with benches in the embrasures. Between the two windows there is an enormous fireplace, 1.4 metres deep, 2 metres wide and 2.3 metres high. Was this the place where they heated the instruments of torture? Across the room from this fireplace two small recesses have been cut into the wall. Carved on the walls there are inscriptions of all kinds, for the most part indecipherable, in writing dating from the 14th century onwards. In the recess nearest the door there is a drawing of a naked woman with here hands tied behind here back to a stake. Crouching in front of her there is a man with a stick raised to strike her. Nearby there is a Christ on the Cross. Viollet-le-Duc cleared out the room on the floor below, which was full of rubbish, and the work engaged in this operation discovered some bones there. There is no staircase leading to this ground floor room. One was obliged to go down through a trap-door in the floor by means of a rope or a ladder. In the middle there is a stone pillar. Chains attached to the pillar lie on the floor. There can be little doubt that this was a cell. Such then is the tower constructed in about 1280 by Philip the Bold. He gave the lower part of the tower, which is close to the episcopal palace, to the bishop. Thus the tower is also known as the «Bishop's Round Tower». We know that at the beginnings of the Inquisition in 1233, the Bishop had direct control over this special court.

Narrowing of the Lists between the Tower of the Inquisition on the right and the Petit Canissou Tower on the left.

1) PETIT CANISSOU TOWER

The Lists narrow appreciably between the two towers. This narrow passageway was a deliberate construction. It was easy to defend and if necessary could be blocked altogether to stop an enemy who had already captured part of the Lists.

2) THE BISHOP'S SQUARE TOWER SEEN FROM THE LISTS

This tower owes its name to the Bishop's Palace which used to be nearby. It is the only one of the towers which straddles the two ramparts. A 13th century tower, it served as an observation post, and the upper platform was intended to receive either a catapult or a mangonel (an engine for casting stones etc.) to riposte to the assaillants' engines of war. The tower has four small observation turrets, called bartizans, one at each corner. Two of these face outwards and two face inwards. This is significant, indicating that the garrison had also to protect itself against a possible attack from the inside.

3) THE GRAND CANISSOU TOWER *(seen from the bishop's square tower)*

Beyond the Bishop's Square Tower the Lists get wider again as they pass between the tall rough-hewn walls which protected the former Bishop's Palace and the relatively low battlements of the Outer Wall. The Grand Canissou Tower built by St. Louis is overlooked by the Cahuzac Tower on the Outer Wall.

4) THE GRAND BURLAS TOWER *(seen from the outer moat)*

The Grand Burlas Tower was constructed with particular care by St. Louis to cover the most exposed point of the Citadel. A large semi-isolated construction it constitutes a break in the sentry-way. The Carcassonne chronicler Besse, who lived in the 17th century, refers to the «Grand Burlas Barbican» so there must once have been an exit at that point.

5) THE MOULIN DU MIDI (SOUTH MILL) TOWER WITH THE MIPADRE TOWER IN THE BACKGROUND

The tower gets its name from the fact that a wind-mill once stood on top of it. On the town side a wide stairway leads down into the large space known as «the St. Nazaire Cloister or Yard». This piece of ground is at present partially occupied by the large open-air theatre of the Citadel where performances are given during the Festival in July.

6) THE ST. NAZAIRE TOWER

Like the Bishop's Tower this tower is square with four turrets. Furthermore it is a complete fortress in itself and could be isolated completely from the nearby sentry-ways. Its possession of a well and an oven completed its self-sufficiency, making it the vigilant guardian of the South Postern cut into the Outer Wall and of the Barbican known as the Cremade Tower.

3 4
5 6

THE MOULIN DU MIDI TOWER

When Viollet-le-Duc restored this tower he did not take the position of the mill into account. This is an opportune moment to explain that one should not attach too much importance to the names given to the towers, which might be named in terms of the use made of them, of things in their vicinity or of some important personnage who lived there. However the existence of mills for the exclusive use of the garrison cannot be disputed, after the appearance of mills in the region during the 13th century. The installation of a mill here seems perfectly natural. There was an oven in each of its neighbours, the Mipadre and St. Nazaire Towers, and water could be supplied to the bakers from the well of the latter tower. In this way the ideal of fortress builders was achieved: a garrison which was completely self-sufficient during a long siege.

THE PRISON TOWER

One can still see in the ground-floor room the holes into which the iron grills in front of the window-slits fitted. The graffiti on the walls are probably the work of prisoners, prisoners however who were not considered dangerous, since they were not deprived of either air or light like those in the Tower of the Inquisition, and what is more they were left in the immediate neighbourhood of a gate opening onto the Citadel.

Top: The Moulin du Midi Tower seen from the Citadel.
Bottom: The Prison Tower.

General view from the south of the Basilica of St. Nazaire and St. Celse.

THE BASILICA OF ST. NAZAIRE

In front of the south transept there is a chapel which was built in the second half of the 13th century, the Radulphe Chapel. One can still see the traces of three arches which formerly constituted part of the «St. Nazaire Cloister or Close» which has since disappeared. There is no proof that such an edifice ever really existed. What disappeared some time before 1792 was probably not a cloistered building but a cloistered way of life. The canons gathered together in this walled enclosure, referred to in a Papal Bull issued by Gregory IX and dated 1226 as the «clausae locorum», while at the same time living in separate houses or cells. They had in common a refectory, a cellar, a sacristy, a kitchen, an infirmary, a quadrangle, a well, stores and granges. All this formed an ensemble known as the Cloister. The Basilica stands behind the chapel. The building can be divided into two parts: the Romanesque Nave dating from the 11th and 12th centuries on the left, and the Gothic Transept and Choir dating from the 13th and 14th centuries on the right. Viollet-le-Duc in his report to the Ministry of Fine Arts stated that the whole of the Citadel was a museum and that its church constituted the jewel of this museum. The Basilica of St. Nazaire and St. Celse, which was a cathedral church until 1801, stands on the site of a former Carolingian cathedral. The fate of the cathedral parallels that of the fortress. As the new town or Lower Town grew in importance so the importance of the Upper Town or Citadel declined. The bishops became more and more used to living in the Lower Town and round about 1745 Bishop Bazin de Bezons put the final seal on this move by installing himself in the vast building which he had had built and which today has become the Hôtel de la Préfecture.

The work on the Romanesque cathedral started towards the end of the 11th century and the church, together with the materials with which it was to be finished, was consecrated by Pope Urban II in June 1096 when he came to preach on the subject of the First Crusade to the Holy Land. The Romanesque church retained its integrity as such as long as Carcassonne retained its independence under the Viscounts. However once the South had been vanquished by the North and the King of France had become master of the Citadel changes also made themselves felt inside. From 1255 to 1266 Carcassonne had as bishop William Radulphe, a Northerner, who was responsible for the Gothic architecture of St. Nazaire.

Balustrade, Modillions and Gargoyles of the gothic part of St. Nazaire seen from the inside of the Citadel.

INSIDE THE BASILICA OF ST. NAZAIRE AND ST. CELSE

On entering the church one is in the presence of an architecture of great austerity. One is faced by a colonnade consisting of square piers flanked by four half-columns and of massive circular pillars. The capitals have various forms of decoration. This is of course the Romanesque Nave which, as has already been pointed out, was started at the end of the 11th century and finished in the 12th. The pillars of the Romanesque Nave divide it into three parts: the centre part of the nave which has a pointed barrel vault, the vaulting having been finished later, and the two aisles which both have semi-circular barrel vaults springing from the same level as the vault of the nave. The aisles are covered with a common ceiling in two sections. The nave consists of six bays. If you walk down the centre of the nave and look towards the sanctuary you are dazzled by the many coloured light radiating from the magnificent stained-glass windows around the apse. This is but a preliminary taste of the sensations which await the visitor to this superb monument.

This Gothic part, which partially replaced the Romanesque Apse, was started in 1269 at which time St. Louis conceded to the Bishop and Chapter «two rods of the street adjacent to the church to repair or found the apse». (A rod was 2 to 3 yards). The work was doubtless directed by northern architects. This union of the Romanesque and Gothic styles is the dominating feature of St. Nazaire. It is not just a simple juxtaposition of two different styles but a careful blending of the styles with the harmony of constrasts symbolizing the union of the «two Frances», the North and the South. The transept and the choir have a pointed arch form and the sanctuary vault looks as if it is supported by the stained-glass windows. There are 22 statues dating from the first quarter of the 14th century attached to the columns of the sanctuary. These represent Christ, the Virgin, the twelve Apostles, six Saints and two Angels. There is an arcade running around the sanctuary, which is roofed by pointed arches supporting the stained-glass windows of the choir. Arches spring from each pillar to a small decorative column set between decorative arches in the walls. They are decorated at both ends with capitals representing the most strange and fantastic subjects: angels holding a censer, others unravelling strips of cloth, men in monks' dress, others with dislocated bodies, yet others with a man's body and an animal head. There is a shepherd playing the bagpipes, a sow feeding her young, birds, snakes, monkeys, calves' heads, foxes and what have you, all of which must certainly have some symbolic significance which, however, escapes us.

The octagonal tower of the gothic part of St. Nazaire seen from inside the Citadel.

The apse of St. Nazaire.

THE APSE OF ST. NAZAIRE (14th CENTURY)

Formed by the development of the transept and the apse, this side of the church is strikingly elegant and gracious. The buttresses are slim and slender as are the mullions separating the windows. The roof of the part in pointed arch form is crowned with a pierced balustrade, the decoration consisting in part of pointed leaf shapes and in part of rounded lobes. Elegant pinnacles crown the buttresses and give the building an overall appearance of lightness. Underneath the cornice there is a row of modillions (projecting brackets under a cornice) representing heads of the most diverse appearances.

WHO WAS ST. NAZAIRE?

Thanks to the «HISTORIA LOMBARDINA», or golden legend, by James de Voraggio, a Dominican born in Genoa round about 1230, we know that Nazaire was the son of Afranius, a Jew of some renown, and of St. Perpetue, a very Christian Roman woman who was baptised by St. Peter himself. Nazaire followed his mother's example and was baptised. Because of the danger of torture and martyrdom which Christians faced, his parents begged him to leave Rome. He left in the company of seven Samaritans, taking with him his parents' riches which he distributed to the poor. His mother who was already dead, appeared to him in a dream and advised him to go to Gaul. Following this advice Nazaire must have crossed the region around Carcassonne, where there are many churches and places bearing his name, before finally reaching Saint-Nazaire on the Atlantic coast. However he was caught and taken back to Nero in chains. Because a child by the name of Celse cried at this spectacle the soldiers rained blows on him and forced him to

Basilica of St. Nazaire: nave and choir.

The Romanesque nave and the organ. ▶

follow them. When Nero saw the two prisoners he ordered them to be thrown into a cell. Subsequently a multitude of wild animals burst into Nero's garden tearing practically everybody to pieces so that Nero, thinking that Nazaire and Celse were the cause of this disaster, ordered his soldiers to get rid of them at any price. The attempt to do away with them failed and the two Saints got as far as Milan, where they were martyred by decapitation.

THE ROMANESQUE NAVE AND THE ORGAN

The organ was already in existence in 1522, having replaced an even older organ. In 1614 the organ had 37 pipes and 7 stops. At the end of the 17th century the organ maker Jean de Joyeuse restored it and put forward a plan to enlarge it. In 1772 Jean-Pierre Cavaille was entrusted with the repair and enlargement of the instrument. He was responsible for putting the present key-board on the front of the organ-loft and introducing pedals. At the end of the 19th century the organ was restored by Michel Roger, organ maker in Bordeaux. The restoration mainly concerned the bellows and the key-board, in which the levers and mechanisms were renewed. The bellows were finally electrified in 1925. Since then the organ has been declared a protected object and necessary restoration will be carried out under the auspices of the Monuments Historiques.

12th CENTURY STOUP (HOLY WATER BASIN)

This stoup consists of a six-sided basin, the sides being cut on the twist, resting on a plinth on top of a twisted column.

BAPTISMAL FONT

The baptismal font is situated at the end of the nave on the right in the chapel of Our Lady of the Good News (Notre-Dame-des-Bonnes-Nouvelles) which was built in 1430 to commemorate the good news of the taking of Orleans by Joan of Arc.

TOMB OF PIERRE DE ROCHEFORT

Against the west wall of St. John's Chapel, formerly called St. Peter's Chapel, which was built by Pierre de Rochefort, Bishop of Carcassonne from 1300 to 1321, is to be found the very interesting monument put up to his memory after his death. The Bishop dressed in full episcopal garb is flanked by two deacons, each of the figures occupying a pointed arch. A succession of priests and monks in procession at their feet no doubt represent the burial service of the pontiff. Pierre de Rochefort is represented standing with his crozier in his left hand. On the round buckle which closes his cope one can see the Pascal Lamb carrying the standard of the Lower Town of Carcassonne. The edges of the cope are embroidered with «rocks checky», the Bishop's arms. His funeral stone is situated in front of the tomb. Statues of St. Peter and St. Paul dating from the 14th century are also to be found in this chapel.

Tomb of Pierre De Rochefort

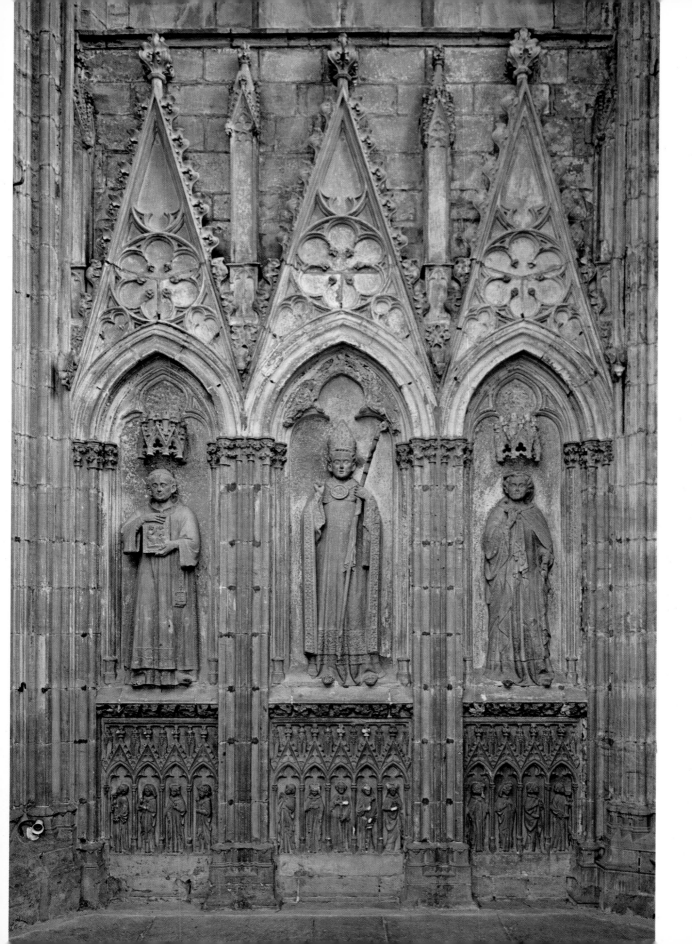

Top: St. Nazaire's Throne, Empire period.

Bottom: Statue of St. Anthony of Padua.

ST. ANTHONY'S CHAPEL

This chapel which was the first on the left on entering the church masked part of a Romanesque portal and so was removed during restoration work. All that remains of it are a low 16th century ogee arch.

THE STAINED-GLASS WINDOWS IN THE CHOIR
from left to right

First window. This is only a grisaille constructed by Viollet-le-Duc from the remains of an 18th century window.

Second window. This 14th century window is divided into two parts: on the left scenes representing the life of St. Peter; on the right scenes from the life of St. Paul. Their respective biographies are to be read from bottom to top.

Third window. This window containing large figures dates from the 16th century. On the left at the bottom the mother of St. Celse presents her son to St. Nazaire. At the top St. Sernin and St. Gimer.

Fourth window. This window filled with small figures is divided into 16 sections and may well be the oldest window of all, dating perhaps from the beginning of the 14th century. It represents 16 scenes from the life of Christ. They are to be read in the sequence bottom left then bottom right and so on.

Fifth window. This 16th century window contains large figures. The two principal subjects are at the bottom the Presentation of the Virgin at the Temple, and, at the top, the Birth of the Virgin.

Sixth window. This 14th century window represents 16 scenes from the life of St. Nazaire and St. Celse. It should be read from bottom to top and from left to right.

Seventh window. Like the first window on the left this is modern.

The stained-glass windows in the Choir.

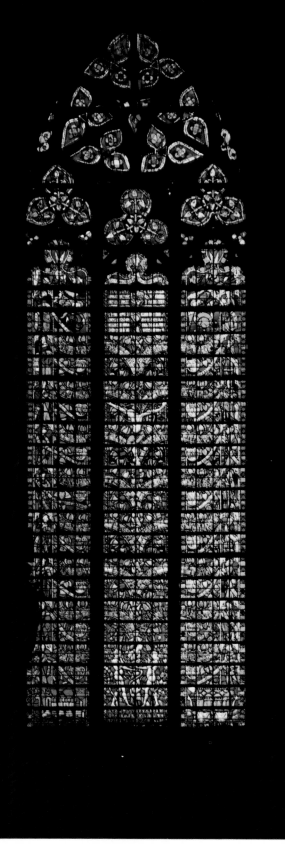

Left: «The tree of life».

Right: «The tree of Jesse».

THE TREE OF LIFE

This 14th century stained-glass window illustrates a text of St. Bonaventure which is inscribed on a pennant running the length of the window. Viollet-le-Duc had the lower part of the window restored by the Parisian painter Gérente who substituted a picture of Adam and Eve surrounded by Noah's Arc and the Arc of the Covenant for the four rivers of Paradise, thus changing the Tree of Life into the Tree of Death. The inscription which follows attempts to correct this error: «*que ligno vetus adam mortem protulit novus adam vitam retulit*». The window is situated in Holy-Cross Chapel on the right of the Choir.

THE TREE OF JESSE

This 14th century window is in the Lady Chapel on the left of the Choir. The upper part of the shows window (the Last Judgement) while the left and right hand sides of the window contain a series of medallions with effigies of 16 prophets. Jesus's family tree does not show all his ancestors. In fact from top to bottom one finds: Jesse, David, Solomon, Roboam, Asa, Josaphat and Joram.

NORTH ROSE WINDOW

This window is older than the South Rose Window and there is little doubt that it dates from the beginning of the 14th century. The main subject is the Queen of Heaven seated on her throne with the Divine Child on her knees. She is surrounded by angels, prophets and saints.

SOUTH ROSE WINDOW

This window also dates from the 14th century and its main subject is Christ in Majesty, Christ teaching with a book in his left hand. Two medallions in the bottom corners of the window show St. Peter and St. Paul. The arms of Pierre de Rochefort, three rocks checky, are shown on either side of Christ.

Top: North Rose Window.

Bottom: South Rose Window.

Top: Recumbent figure of Bishop Géraud du Puy.

A 16th century
Pietà of unkown
origin occupies a
niche in the St.
Anne Chapel. Note
the expression on
the face of the
Virgin.

THE TRINITY

This is a 14th
century stone
Trinity. God the
Father is seated.
The Holy Ghost is
represented by a
dove issuing from
his mouth and joins
him to the Son who
is on the Cross.

RECUMBENT FIGURE OF BISHOP GERAUD DU PUY

On the right of the Lady Chapel beneath a richly ornamented pointed arch there is a bishop's tomb, probably that of Géraud du Puy, Bishop of Narbonne, who died round about 1420. The statue is of alabaster and the prelate is represented lying down with his feet on a lion.

◀ *Bottom*: The Seige Stone.

THE SEIGE STONE

This is the term which has come to be used to designate this strange bas-relief which in fact appears to be part of a sarcophagus. The stone is attached to a wall of the St. Lawrence Chapel which was built in 1324 by Bishop Pierre de Rodier. It shows a seige but although the stone is known to belong to the first half of the 13th century, it has never been clear if it is the 1209 or the 1240 seige of Carcassonne, or even the 1218 seige of Toulouse in which Simon de Montfort died.

Pietà.

The Trinity.

ST. ANNE (terracotta).

Notre-Dame de la Santé (Our Lady of Health) terracotta.

North side of the transept in St. Nazaire.

South side of the transept in St. Nazaire.

The Upper Lists. La Vade Tower ▶

THE UPPER LISTS

A walk through the Lists is an indispensable part of a visit to the Inner Wall. Indeed it is only when one walks about at the foot of the towers that one realizes the way in which each period took advantage of what its predecessors had done while at the same time using new defensive methods. If you go out of the Narbonne Gate and turn right before the drawbridge you will find yourself in the Upper Lists, the space between the Inner and Outer Walls. The first tower on the right is the Tower of the Sacraire de St. Sernin in which you can see the Gothic Window of the former church. The second tower on the right is the Trauquet Tower and immediately after there is a square building which used to enclose a stairway leading down to an underground cellar be-

neath the Lists. This large underground room served as a redoubt in case of a retreat or an attack and could house up to 40 soldiers. From this redoubt one could come out in the outer moat by passing through the postern of the La Peyre Tower which is the first tower on the left in the photo. The third tower on the right is the St. Lawrence Tower, followed by the Davejean Tower which has some large blocks of stone dating from the Roman period set into it in the middle. The last tower on the right in the photo is the Balthazar Tower which dates from the end of the 13th century and is characterized by its rough-hewn stone. It faces the La Vade Tower. Following the Pyrenean Treaty of 1659, as a result of which the Citadel lost its strategic and military importance, this side of the Lists filled up with hovels which Viollet-le-Duc had demolished when he restored it.

Top right: Balthazar Tower.

Top left: Le Trauquet Tower.

Bottom: La Peyre Tower seen from the drawbridge.

LA VADE TOWER

This tower is a true keep or donjon and was one of the first buildings constructed by St. Louis. When he built the Outer Wall towards the middle of the 13th century the La Vade Tower, which was originally isolated, was incorporated into it. Built on rock it has five floors with chimneys, an oven, latrines and a well approximately 26 metres deep. Its name comes from the Languedoc word «bada» meaning «look». Indeed from the top of the tower one can see the only point which overlooks the Citadel. A postern gives access to the outer moat. This was the head-quarters of the «Mortes-Payes», an elite company founded by St. Louis and consisting originally of 220 men. The office of morte-paye was hereditary and perpetual, hence its name. The head of the company was the Provost or Constable but its real chief was the king. Every Sunday they assembled for cross-bow practice in the Lists, a wooden model of a bird placed at the top of one of the towers being the target. The La Vade Tower overlooks a good part of the outer moat.

Tresau Tower on the right and Berard Tower on the left.

THE TRESAU OR TREASURE TOWER

This tower reinforces the defences at the Narbonne Gate and is undoubtedly one of the most beautiful in the Citadel. It is 30 metres high including the pinnacle and has walls 4 metres thick. Seen from inside the Citadel the tower has a somewhat Flemish appearance with its gable and two watch turrets. It got its name because it was used by the Royal Treasury. Like its neighbours, the Narbonne Towers, it dates from the end of the 13th century.

THE TOWER OF THE CONSTABLE'S MILL

This tower is the earliest of the old Romanesque towers which have survived on this side. It was altered in the 12th century and of course its battlements date from the 19th century. The semi-dome vault which supports the first floor dates from the feudal period. A plan dating from 1467 shows a mill fixed on top of the tower. It is claimed that the Constable commanding the «Mortes-Payes» had a private house in the Citadel. Possibly this house was near the tower which bears his name.

THE LA MARQUIERE TOWER

This tower is part of the old Gallo-Roman wall which was used as a foundation for new construction at the time of St. Louis. Like its neighbours it has all the characteristics of a Roman tower constructed at the time of the Barbarian invasions. Semi-circular on the part facing outwards, flat on the town side, it is built with courses of small stones, lines of red brick being used to re-establish or maintain the level. Its base is unbroken up to the level of the curtain and its first floor communicates with the sentry-way by means of two doors which can be barricaded readily. There are no

Top: Tower of the Constable's Mill.

Bottom: La Marquiere Tower.

The Rodez Postern, the Samson Tower and the Avar Mill Tower.

arrow-slits but there were three semi-circular windows facing the outside.

PART OF THE GALLO-ROMAN SIDE OF THE INNER WALL

The Rodez Postern Gate on the north side is a 13th century construction which probably replaced the old Roman Gate. The two towers shown in the photo are typically Gallo-Roman but with some 13th century alterations and 19th century restoration. The most numerous fragments (of the Inner Wall) from the Gallo-Roman period occur in the north and north-west sectors. On the west side the curtains are only 4.5 to 6 metres high because of the escarpment of the hill on this side. Elsewhere their height is 7 to 8 metres. The towers are relatively close to each other having been conceived with the range of the long-bow and of projectile throwing arms in mind. From the time of St. Louis on, the distance between towers could be doubled because of the entry into general use of the cross-bow.

The way up to the Aude gate on the west side of the Citadel.

THE WEST SIDE OF THE CITADEL

The west side of the Citadel is the only side which has natural defences: the steep slope, which can be seen in the photo, and the river Aude which formerly flowed much closer to the hillside. Nevertheless, even on this side the defences have been increased. The relatively modern road which climbs up from the Faubourg de la Barbacane to the Aude Gate makes a sharp left turn in the direction of the castle and leads into the enormous fortified enclosure of which a brief description has already been given on page 30. The walls of this enclosure merit special attention. First of all on entering the enclosure one sees a small guard post on the right which was doubtless roofed over in the past. Behind this post an ogival gate, called the «Seneschal's Gate», opens towards the southwest and leads to the Upper Lists after passing under a tall cross-wall. This formidable battlemented wall, which blocks two exits at once had a double scope: it stopped any attack coming from the Barbican road to the Aude Gate and it prevented any attack from the Lists. The curtain which starts on the left is crowned with a battlement, and this increases in height with the wall and the ground. A sentry-way whose successive levels are linked by ladders permitted defenders to reach the curtains. The Inner Wall on the right is even higher. It was therefore necessary to foresee the eventuality that, assaillants having penetrated into the fortified enclosure, the defenders would have to fall back within the Inner Wall. A gate on the right with its threshhold «suspended in the air» so to speak, served this purpose without it being necessary to open the gate behind which a stairway leads to the Aude Gate proper. In the enclosure on the left is a block of stone which marks the position of a cistern whose entrance is cut into the curtain itself. This reminds us of the problem of water supplies. We already know that lack of water was fatal to Raymond-Roger Trencavel, drought having dried up the wells and the cisterns in August 1209. But above all according to the Song of the Crusade the Citadel was defeated «because they had been deprived of the water called Aude». This then is the only chink in the Citadel's armour, the only defect which the king's engineers were impotent to remedy completely even though they did sink several more wells inside the Citadel. The Romans, past masters in the art, seem to have found several springs on the hill at Pech-Mary to the east of the Citadel and to have led the waters back to the town by means of an aqueduct whose remains were seen by Cros-Meyrevieille. Today the Citadel has 22 wells and cisterns including the two public wells: the big well and the Plo well.

THE 14th OF JULY, THE BURNING OF THE CITADEL

Flames pierce the darkness and suddenly the Citadel seems to be burning in a thousand places. Has the Black Prince returned with the intention this time of burning down the Citadel? Is it the end of the world, with billowing clouds of smoke and flashes of flame? Rockets are exploding on all sides. Are those sounds we hear cries of distress and calls for help, or are they the sounds of arms going off and of catapults launching their mortal charges? Does the smoke come from the fires heating up the cauldrons of boiling oil and molten lead? This is the hour when the Citadel stands in the midst of the blood shed in its defence and for its survival. If we give free rein to our imaginations, we can see ghosts rising out of these magical stones: Raymond-Roger Trencavel, Simon de Montfort, St. Louis, Philip the Bold. The past presents itself before the eyes of those who know how to see it.

The burning of the Citadel.

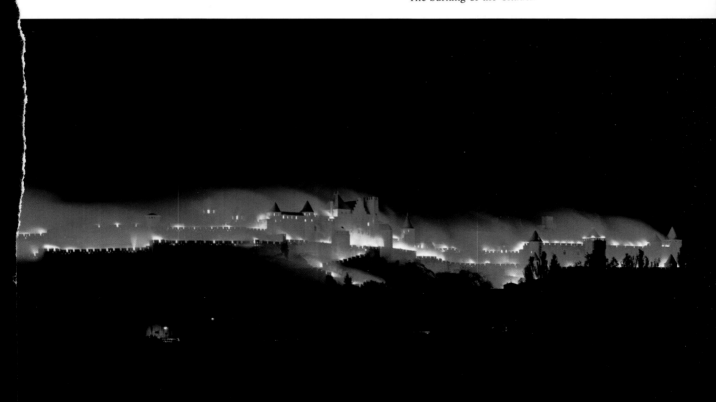

INDEX